BEAR CREEK LIBRARY

D0099752

DISCARD

DISCARD

COUNTRIES IN THE NEWS

ISRAEL

Kieran Walsh

Rourke

Publishing LLC

Vero Beach, Florida 32964

956.94
W

© 2004 Rourke Publishing LLC

All rights reserved. No part of this book may be reproduced or utilized in any form or by any means, electronic or mechanical including photocopying, recording, or by any information storage and retrieval system without permission in writing from the publisher.

www.rourkepublishing.com

The country's flag is correct at the time of going to press.

PHOTO CREDITS:
All images © Peter Langer Associated Media Group

Title page: A view of the southern resort of Eilat.

Editor: Frank Sloan

Cover and interior design by Nicola Stratford

Library of Congress Cataloging-in-Publication Data

Walsh, Kieran.
  Israel / Kieran Walsh.
    p. cm. — (Countries in the news)
Includes bibliographical references and index.
Contents: Welcome to Israel — The people — Life in Israel — School and sports — Food and holidays — The future — Fast facts — The Muslim world.
  ISBN 1-58952-679-1 (hardcover)
  1. Israel—Juvenile literature. 2. Israel—Description and travel—Juvenile literature. [1. Israel.] I. Title. II. Series.

  DS118.W355 2003
  956.94—dc21

                                        2003005669

Printed in the USA

CG/CG

BEAR CREEK LIBRARY
Bend, Oregon

5053

TABLE OF CONTENTS

WELCOME TO
ISRAEL

Israel is a small country at the eastern end of the Mediterranean Sea. This is where Europe, Africa, and Asia come together. This part of the world is known as the Middle East.

Israel became a country in 1948, when it was set up as a homeland for the Jewish people.

The caves at Qumram, where the Dead Sea Scrolls were found

For a long time, the land was known as Palestine. During, that time, Arabs and Jews shared the land, as they do today. But sharing the land isn't easy.

Israel is about 300 miles (480 kilometers) long, and it is very narrow. The country is about the same size as the state of New Jersey.

Much of Israel is dry land. The Negev Desert is in the south and covers about half of the country. The Dead Sea is in the east. It is really a lake that is 1,300 feet (400 meters) below sea level.

Israel's most famous city is Jerusalem. Jewish people go to Jerusalem's Old City to the Wailing Wall, where they pray. **Muslims** go to the Dome of the Rock. This is a **mosque**, a place where Muslims pray. Christians also visit Jerusalem.

The Wailing Wall in Jerusalem, where Jews go to pray

THE PEOPLE

People who live in Israel are known as **Israelis**. Five out of six people who live there are Jewish. Only about one million people who live in Israel are not Jewish. They are Arabs, and most of the Arabs in Israel are Muslims.

An Israeli born in Israel is known as a **sabra**. Sabra is a **Hebrew** word that means "prickly pear."

A young Jewish boy prays at the Wailing Wall.

Orthodox Jews gather at a cemetery in Jerusalem.

Most Israelis live in cities. Some people, however, live on farms. A farm in Israel is known as a **kibbutz**. People who live there share the work. They may also live together and raise their children together.

Because there is not much water in the country, people have to **irrigate** the land in order for crops to grow. Citrus fruit and melons have become important crops. Israel does not have many **natural resources**.

*Most of the fruit sold at markets in Israel
is grown in the country.*

LIFE IN
ISEAEL

People come from all over the world to visit Israel. Because, of this, many Israelis work in the tourist industry. Jews, Christians, and Muslims all come to see the sights that are important to their history.

One of Israel's most popular tourist attractions is at Masada.

Jewish men and women between 18 and 21 have to serve in the army. Because of the troubles between Arabs and Jews, being in the army is an important part of life in Israel.

BEAR CREEK LIBRARY
Bend, Oregon

The Dome of the Rock in Jerusalem is a mosque where many Muslims go to worship.

SCHOOL AND SPORTS

Children must go to school from the time they are five until they are 16. Some of the schools are run by the state. Some are Jewish religious schools. They are known as **yeshivas**. There are also Arab schools. There are many colleges and universities in Israel.

! Swimming is a popular sport because the weather is so nice in Israel. Soccer and basketball are the most popular team sports. Israelis also enjoy hiking, bicycling, and camping.

A young boy reads a book while floating in the Dead Sea.

FOOD AND HOLIDAYS

The people of Israel eat many different kinds of food. Some Jewish people observe **kosher** laws. This means, among other things, that they may not eat dairy and meat products at the same meal. Arabs eat **falafel**, which is a paste made of chick peas and oil.

There are Jewish, Muslim, and Christian holidays. The Jewish day of worship is the Sabbath. It begins at sundown on Friday and lasts until sundown Saturday. Other holidays include **Passover**, **Rosh Hashanah**, and **Yom Kippur**.

Christians come to Israel to celebrate Christmas and Easter.

Muslims celebrate **Ramadan**. During this month-long holiday Muslims **fast** all day. At the end of Ramadan, Mulsims celebrate with a holiday known as **Id ul Fitr**.

16

Christians go to Jerusalem's Church of the Holy Sepulchre on many occasions.

Another view of Eilat, where many visitors to Israel spend their leisure time.

THE FUTURE

The future of Israel is bright. The young country is growing, and so are its resources. Fruit is a major crop, which grows better because of irrigation. There is enough fruit to **export**, which brings money to Israel.

Israel's biggest concern, however, is peace. Jews and Muslims believe the country should belong to each other. They are struggling to find a solution. And many people all over the world are trying to help Israel find peace.

FAST FACTS

Area: 7,800 square miles
(20,200 square kilometers)

Borders: Lebanon, Syria,
West Bank, Jordan, Egypt

Population: 6,029,529
Monetary Unit: new shekel

Largest Cities: Tel Aviv (2,001,000);
Jerusalem (661,000); Haifa (255,300)
Government: Republic

Religion: 80% Jewish; 15% Sunni Muslims
Crops: citrus fruit, vegetables, cotton

Natural Resources: copper, phosphates,
bromide, clay, potash
Major Industries: Hi-tech design and manufactures,
wood and paper products, food and beverages

MUSLIMS IN ISRAEL

Although there are 1,200,000,000 Muslims worldwide, only about 1,000,000 Muslims live in Israel. They live side by side with the Jewish people, and they don't always live in peace.

There are two parts of the land of Israel that are disputed. These are the West Bank and the Gaza Strip (see map on page 5). These pieces of land are claimed by Israel, but most of the people who live there are Muslims. This has caused a lot of difficulty in recent times.

GLOSSARY

export (ECKS port) — a product that is sent out of the country

falafel (fuh LAH ful) — a paste made of chick peas and oil

fast (FAST) — to give up food, usually for religious reasons

Hebrew (HEE BREW) — the language of the Jewish people

Id ul Fitr (ID UHL FIT ur) — a holiday celebrated at the end of Ramadan

Irrigate (ir uh GAYT) — to provide water for growing crops

Israelis (IZZ ray leez) — people who live in Israel

kibbutz (KIB BOOTZ) — a farm in Israel

kosher (KOH shur) — dietary laws of the Jewish people

mosque (MOSK) — a Muslim place of worship

Muslims (MUZ lumz) — people who follow the religion of Islam

natural resources (NAT you ruhl RE sor sez) — products found or grown in a place

Passover (PASS oh vur) — a holiday that celebrates when the Jewish people were freed from slavery from Egypt

Ramadan (RAM uh DAN) — the ninth month of the Muslim year

Rash Hashanah (ROSH Hah shawn uh) — the Jewish New Year

sabra (SAW bruh) — a native-born Israeli

yeshiva (yuh SHEE vuh) — a Hebrew school

Yom Kippur (YAWM KIP POOR) — a Jewish holiday of atonement celebrated with fasting and prayers

FURTHER READING

Find out more about Israel with these helpful books:

- Fisher, Frederick and Ken Chang. *Israel.* Gareth Stevens, 2000

- Italia, Bob. *Israel.* Abdo, 2001

- Park, Ted. *Taking Your Camera to Israel.* Steadwell Books, 2001

WEBSITES TO VISIT

- www.mfa.gov.il/mfa/home.asp

- www.goisrael.com/

INDEX

About the Author

Kieran Walsh is a writer of children's nonfiction books, primarily on historical and social studies topics. A graduate of Manhattan College, in Riverdale, NY, his degree is in Communications. Walsh has been involved in the children's book field as editor, proofreader, and illustrator as well as author.